JOHN BERRYMAN

Poems selected by

MICHAEL HOFMANN

ff

faber and faber

First published in 2004
by Faber and Faber Limited
3 Queen Square London WC1N 3AU

Photoset by Wilmaset Ltd, Birkenhead, Wirral
Printed in England by Bookmarque Ltd, Croydon

A CIP record for this book
is available from the British Library

ISBN 0–571–21781–8

10 9 8 7 6 5 4 3 2 1

Michael Hofmann was born in Freiburg, Germany, in 1957. He has published four collections of poetry, most recently *Approximately Nowhere* (1999). His selected prose, *Behind the Lines*, was published in 2001.

Contents

Introduction

In geometry there is a word secant, for a line that enters a circle at some oblique, imprevisable angle, slices through it, and leaves it again, and that to me is what John Berryman is like in American poetry: a sort of one-off comet that approached that cosy solar system, lit it up for a while, and then exited. A passing glory, giving one a sense of distance, disorderliness and unconventional possibilities, and leaving behind deeper darkness, humdrum and disapproval. Certainly, you couldn't make him up, any more than you could one of Tambo's crushing asides to Bones in *The Dream Songs*.

Like the comet, Berryman was to be seen coming for a long time before he actually 'arrived'. Born in 1914, he did not publish his first full-length book, *The Dispossessed*, until 1948, and it was only in 1953 that he graduated from the realms of the 'promising' – horizon status – with his long poem, *Homage to Mistress Bradstreet*; and it was not until the appearance of 77 *Dream Songs* in 1964, when he was fifty, that he established a poetic identity, and achieved enduring renown. That, at the same time, was his zenith, his moment of maximum visibility and brilliance. The following year, he won the Pulitzer Prize. In 1967, he published *Berryman's Sonnets* (an account of an adulterous love affair written twenty years previously and never published before) and a retrospective *Short Poems*. In 1968, he published *His Toy, His Dream, His Rest*, a selection of a further 308 Dream Songs (four times the number of the original volume, and nowhere near as innovative). For this he was given the National Book Award in 1969. *The Dream Songs* were then published in one volume – 385, count them – and they were followed by a couple of chatty, rather prosy, sporadically highly attractive books, with earthy and heavenly sections, *Love and Fame* (1970) and *Delusions, etc.* (1972). By the time *Delusions* appeared, it was posthumous, for on 7 January 1972 Berryman had killed himself by leaping from

Washington Bridge, Minneapolis (where he lived and taught) on to the frozen banks of the Mississippi. One further posthumous selection was put together by John Haffenden, called *Henry's Fate and Other Poems* (1978); disappointingly but not altogether surprisingly, it contained many pieces in the Dream Song mode, and a lot of naked distress, including an account, written apparently forty-eight hours before his death, of a rehearsal or dry-run for it: 'I didn't. And I didn't. Sharp the Spanish blade...' In the decade or so after his death, there was a little spate of critical attention – much of it again from John Haffenden, who also wrote the best biography of the poet (*The Life of John Berryman*, Routledge, 1982) – but recently, although *The Dream Songs* have continued to sell, at least in the States, things have gone rather quiet around Berryman. Space has closed up again, and darkened.

I may of course be mistaken about both, but while I find it quite easy to think of Sylvia Plath without and apart from her suicide, I can't do that with Berryman. It was a part of him for longer, and it's harder to think what else he might have done. The long doldrums of his life, and the impatience for eternity evinced in his rapid clustering of publications, both suggest that he never found any sort of stable rhythm for a creative life. Further, the poetic creed I believe he really did espouse, the so-called 'extremism' – more of this later – would have tended to disable whatever self-protective or life-prolonging mechanisms he did have. Beyond that, belonging as he did (he was its spokesman, its shop steward) to what always seemed to be a very consciously formulated generation, the one after Eliot and Pound – other members of which also ended badly or early, like Plath, like Jarrell, like Roethke, like Schwartz – the one of which Lowell wrote drolly, in his late poem 'For John Berryman'; '*Les Maudits* – the compliment/ each American generation/ pays itself in passing,' it was a fixture in his thought. One Dream Song, #172, (not included here) begins: 'Your face broods from my table, Suicide'; another, #153, goes:

> I'm cross with god who has wrecked this generation.
> First he seized Ted, then Richard, Randall, and now
>   Delmore.
> In between he gorged on Sylvia Plath.
> That was a first-rate haul. He left alive
> fools I could number like a kitchen knife
> but Lowell he did not touch.

(The weirdly tactless, *mal a propos*, all-but-ambivalent reference to Lowell is typical of Berryman at a certain point.)

Stronger than all of these, however, was the pull on Berryman of his father's example. John Allyn Smith (the poet carried the same name; Berryman was a stepfather) was a sort of itinerant banker, who took the family around Oklahoma, and then down to Florida; in 1926, from an accumulation of personal and business reasons, he shot himself, having previously threatened to swim out and drown himself with his son. (This terrible episode haunted Berryman all his life; at low moments, he kept returning to it; it makes an appearance in Dream Songs #143 and #145, where incidentally, the 'Whitman on his tower' is not – or at least is not primarily – the poet, but a Texan mass killer, Charles Whitman.) Yet another Dream Song, #34, 'My mother has your shotgun,' touches on the suicide of Ernest Hemingway, whose father, ominously for Berryman, had also shot himself. Suicide was not merely in front of him – one among several possibilities, his ultimate, randomly taken choice – but to the front and the rear and both sides.

This combination of factors – frustration, delay, ambition, self-destructiveness – to me seems to set Berryman on a kind of personal rampage through life and literature. His own and others', they were conflated and confused, and used as tokens in a kind of mortal spree. His progress is alternately too slow and too rapid. Asked in his *Paris Review* interview by Peter Stitt about Eliot (characteristically, it was conducted as late as 1970, and also appeared posthumously), he replied:

I now rate him very high. I think he is one of the greatest poets who ever lived. Only sporadically good. What he would do – he would collect himself and write a masterpiece, then relax for several years writing prose, earning a living, and so forth; then he'd collect himself and write another masterpiece, very different from the first, and so on. He did this about five times, and after the *Four Quartets* he lived on for twenty years. Wrote absolutely nothing. It's a very strange career. Very – a pure system of spasms. My career is like that. It is horribly like that.

The self-aggrandizing movement from Eliot to himself, the uncomfortably visceral words 'horrible' and 'spasms', the vertiginously apt term 'career' – he might as well have said 'plummet' – all suggest that literature was not finally going to be able to contain Berryman, any more than life. (Evidently, he had no appetite for 'writing prose, earning a living, and so forth', much less for twenty years of writing 'absolutely nothing'.) Lowell wrote of him, with demure horror commingled with awe: 'As he became more inspired and famous and drunk, more and more John Berryman, he became less good company and more a happening – slashing eloquence in undertones, amber tumblers of bourbon, a stony pyramid talking down a rugful of admirers.' Saul Bellow, in an exquisitely insightful piece (one of the best accounts, not just of a poet, but of another human being I have ever read), recalls:

I would visit John at an institution [...] called, I believe, The Golden Valley. He was not there because he had broken his leg. The setting of The Golden Valley was indeed golden. It was early autumn, and the blond stubble fields shone. John's room was furnished simply. On the floor was the straw *tatami* mat on which he performed his Yoga exercises. At a collapsible bridge table he wrote Dream Songs. He said, 'As you can see, they keep me in a baby crib. They raise the sides at night to keep me from falling out. It is humiliating!

Listen, pal, I have written something new. It is,' he reassured me, raising hands that shook, 'Absolutely a knockout!'

He put a finger to the bridge of his glasses, for nothing was steady here. Things shook and dropped. Inside and outside they wavered and flew. The straw of Golden Valley swirled on the hills.

John had waited a long time for this poet's happiness. He had suffered agonies of delay. Now came the poems. They were killing him.

This is the poet as psycho-pharmaceutical centrifuge, as astral phenomenon. It's strange to think of him for so long as buttoned up and repressed and preppy and clean-shaven and starchy, small, rather shifty eyes, blue jaws, a middle-manager with a secret penchant for golf; and then with the beard – the badge of his emancipation and loss of control – in Terence Spencer's magnificent photographs of him in 1967 in Ireland, hunched over, possessed, in spate, the beard gesticulating and waving like a third hand. The one purse-lipped and Anglo-Saxon and mute, the other an uncontrollably gabby sage. From an unhealthy tightness to an unhealthy looseness.

Berryman was of the first generation of American 'professional poets', the prizes, the residencies, the summer schools, the readings, (the first creative writing department established at the University of Iowa by Paul Engle in 1947), but never entirely in it. He thought about it a lot, the biz, poe-business, sometimes drily, often in a sour or jaundiced way: about publication and publications, success, fame, tribulations, colleagues and rivals. (There cannot be another poet who mentions the *Times Literary Supplement* in his poems as often as Berryman does.) He was an eager participant all right, and very ambitious, but seems on the whole to have been what the Germans call *ein Zaungast*, 'a fence-guest', semi-excluded by a mixture of luck, tardiness, unsuitability and being stuck out in the Midwest. The decisive development in the latter half of the twentieth century was the entry of literature into the academy. Poetry became something that was taught, and the people who taught it, as often as not, were the poets. (There are very few and very significant exceptions to this professionalization of poetry in America: Elizabeth Bishop until the very end of her life, James Schuyler, Frederick Seidel.) Berryman, though, was not part of that influx, that rush to be on the reservation or given one's tenured cage, he was an old-fashioned poet-scholar. He didn't 'teach writing'; he was, by analogy with the 'legitimate theatre', a legitimate university man. Peter Stitt puts it to him: 'You once said: "I masquerade as a writer. Actually I am a scholar",' and Berryman says:

> Housman is one of my heroes and always has been. He was a detestable and miserable man. Arrogant, unspeakably lonely, cruel, and so on, but an absolutely marvelous minor poet, I think, and a great scholar. And I'm about *equally* interested in those two activities. In him they are perfectly distinct. You are dealing with an absolute schizo-phrenic. In me they seem closer together.

(See Dream Song #205 on Housman, where he says 'he was a fork/ saved by his double genius and certain emendations'.)

Had he lived at an earlier time – say, Housman's time – Berryman's life would have been literature. It is his apprentice-ship to his teacher Mark Van Doren, his having tea with Yeats at the Athenaeum and lighting 'the great man's cigarette', his passionate friendship with Delmore Schwartz and his joshing buddiness with Dylan Thomas (his senior by a single day, 'born one day before I surfaced' and the subject of the late poem 'In Memoriam 1914–1953'), his many elegies for con-temporaries and coevals, his difficult awe and envy of Lowell, his imposing reading and scholarship. As it is, I think he lived in the uncomfortable crack between literature and institutions. He divided himself among the three activities of poet, scholar and teacher – hence the instability of his interview replies on Eliot, and on Housman. It was a perpetual round of paper-scissors-stone. At one time, he promised to be a great

Shakespearean editor (a book, *Shakespeare's Understanding*, was assembled, again by John Haffenden, from his notes and drafts). His gifts as a teacher were such as to draw from the American poet, Philip Levine, the following passionate testimonial (from a semester where Berryman did once teach writing at Iowa):

> ... the workshop and the night class in poetry were the best classes I've ever been a part of – John was a great teacher & he gave so fucking much of himself & there was so much in him that it was amazing. Amazing ... We loved him; it was the middle of the shittiest part of American life, the Rosenbergs had just been murdered, Joe McCarthy was king, and John could make the study of poetry, our god damned mediocre poetry, the center of the world.

Now – in *The Dream Songs*, say, or in the Princeton of *Berryman's Sonnets*, or the Cambridge of *Love and Fame* – life reasserts itself, now literature, now teaching. 'I'll teach Luke,' the poem 'On Suicide' ends. The last note of *Berryman's Sonnets* is 'I sat down & wrote.' 'Venice, 182–', about Lord Byron, is an extremely powerful and intimate close-up.

Berryman performed this sort of triangular, or tri-axial, rotation even as he flew across the night sky of American poetry. Certainly, it was exorbitant, and a kind of exhaustion and coarseness did finally set in. The later Dream Songs are a falling-off, and the two subsequent books, *Love and Fame* and *Delusions, etc.*, both exhibit a revealing disintegrative fission between the human and the divine (the two aspects of Berryman that Lowell beautifully described as 'riot' and 'prayer'), one book closing with 'Eleven Addresses to the Lord', the other beginning with 'Opus Dei'. The rotation was slowing down. In its place came the terrible, scandalous confusion he articulated in the *Paris Review* interview:

> My idea is this: the artist is extremely lucky who is presented with the worst possible ordeal which will not actually kill

him. At that point, he's in business. Beethoven's deafness, Goya's deafness, Milton's blindness, that kind of thing. And I think that what happens in my poetic work in the future will probably largely depend not on my sitting calmly on my ass as I think, 'Hmm, hmm, a long poem again? Hmm,' but on being knocked in the face, and thrown flat, and given cancer, and all kinds of other things short of senile dementia. At that point, I'm out, but short of that, I don't know. I hope to be nearly crucified.

As a philosophy of creation, this is repellently mistaken (why the exemption, one wonders, of senile dementia?), but it comes out of the collapse of Berryman's spinning triangle, now reduced to one morbid, metastasizing point. It's a doped athlete speaking, not a poet (the shared and cynical distortion produced by professionalism). It's hardly surprising that, just before, Berryman states his conviction 'that endowment is a very small part of achievement. I would rate it about fifteen or twenty percent.' He sounds like a sports coach.

This, Berryman's sorry legacy, has left its shadow over him and his reputation. Poetry, in his practice of it, came to seem a sickly and a recklessly dangerous occupation; one might as well go pot-holing or rock-climbing. The card-carrying careerism of his successors (but note also the expression of Berryman himself, 'At that point, he's in business') comes to seem reasonable, though still not attractive. The malicious and unerring Auden claimed the existence of a suicide note; it read 'Your move, Cal [Lowell].' When I came to my tutor with the intention of writing a long undergraduate essay on *Berryman's Sonnets*, back in 1978, his opening question to me was: 'Are you interested in suicide?'

Accordingly, any selection of Berryman has, to some extent, to oppose itself to the worst tendencies of the poet. There will be a little denial in it, and a little false innocence. Still, always better that than the lurid, macabre, self-complacent and self-destructive message that he mistakenly proclaimed at the end. There is, luckily, enough else to choose from.

My selection begins with 'A Professor's Song' from a little sequence of proto-Dream Song monologues called 'The Nervous Songs', the one piece I have chosen to keep from Berryman's starchy and derivative beginnings. Both the *Sonnets* – which make up about a fifth of the present book – and *Homage to Mistress Bradstreet*, here excerpted – lend themselves to being read as further docking manoeuvres with literature on the part of the learned and aware poet. The *Dream Songs* – three-fifths of my total – show the antic dance of the poet, scholar, teacher and all-round 'human American man' at its best. Berryman's style – Lowell after his death admitted 'I'm afraid I mistook it for forcing, when he came into his own' – breaks other components into a fantastic, *inoui* new whole. It encompasses all his literariness, his versedness, I would like to call it. Lowell in his earlier bafflement referred deprecatingly to 'babytalk', Michael Schmidt compares it to cummings, 'but a cummings carrying a huge library on his back', but the best is probably Adrienne Rich, noting that 'Shakespeare's English and some minstrelly refrain meet, salute and inform each other', before going on to wonder: 'The English (American) language. Who knows entirely what it is? Maybe two men in this decade: Bob Dylan, John Berryman.'

This knowledge is there already in the *Sonnets* and the *Bradstreet*, but chiefly it illuminates the *Dream Songs*, which seem to me to be written with as much freedom, and – before a manner, a *tic*, could establish itself – as much necessity as anything I can think of. 'Write as short as you can, in order, of what matters,' is the order Berryman famously gave his guild and himself, but that, I am tempted to say, was later, when the idea of poetry as a nailed-on straitjacket was being promulgated. I love the extremes of courtliness and creatureliness in *The Dream Songs*, on the one hand such things as 'Come away, Mr Bones' (#77) (the occasion for Adrienne Rich's first rapture), or 'There is a kind of undetermined hair,/ half-tan, extraordinary getaway or liftoff – the poem is a bristling and dazzling display of grammar: almost one's first thoughts on seeing it are to do with agreements and ('here airless') appositionals! The first 'here', which Henry (or Berryman) is in such a hurry to quit, is the world, a world, further, in which the world (or something very similar – an apple, or a green apple, or perhaps Snow White's poisoned – 'witchy' – apple) falls into your lap, but without making you any the happier for it. The poem revisits the theme of (whose?) 'How pleasant it is to have money, heigh-ho' or Brecht's '*Lied von der belebenden Wirkung des Geldes*', but in an agnostic or unsatisfied mode, the mode, if you like, of Midas, or, worse, a Midas with a paper touch. It is a poem of accursedness or ill-fortune, set up as in a parallel world (the world of depression, or perhaps a mirror-world, which would help to account for the role of the mirror at the end of the poem in breaking the spell?) similar, say, to the 'vast landscape of Lament' in Rilke's Tenth Elegy ('*einst waren wir reich*' – 'we used to be rich'). From 'whence', from 'departed', from 'airless', from 'that witchy ball' and 'green living', I have a sense that the earliest Russian and American space missions – Gagarin in 1961 – may have played into the poem, and the very earliest satellite photographs of ourselves – mirrorings – from space. If one strand of the poem's thought is cosmic, the other is monetary; it is there in the play on 'interest', 'living' and 'green' – with its echo of the American dollar, the 'greenback' – and the spectacular 'Figurez-vous'. This sort of image-cluster is something Berryman learned from Shakespeare, who is a constant pressure on his style. Typically, such literariness and ambition are balanced by an early use of the illiterate particle 'like'. The verbs are conspicuously loose-fitting and vitalist: 'drops', 'swarms', 'sheds' and 'eaten'. It is out of the vegetable nature of these that the animal character of 'gentle friendly Henry Pussy-cat' is compounded. 'Stillwater' in the third stanza is a penitentiary in Oklahoma (Berryman, as one would have suspected, actually owned such a mirror); and 'plink' is a bit of family slang. There is no one else in the poem but Henry: it is he who smiles, who is 'alone', then 'desolate', and finally triumphant. Still, the very clever introduction of the murderer as it were flavours the poem (Berryman identified his particular area of expertise as a poet as the personal pronoun!). The murderer brings in society, depth, risk, an alter ego. The poem is an authentic 'Dream Song', diffusely coercive, unconventional, complex, bleak, tender in adversity, rallying.

The *Dream Songs* vary through every degree of lucidity and opacity, some of them, beautifully, add up (#188, #308), many others are at least consistent in their gestures (#40, #91, #379), a few leave unanswered difficulties (#3, #28), but almost all – and I hope all those here – make their own distinct mark on silence and the page. They are dramatic poems – few more so. Often, they end up in rhetorical reaches most poems don't go near: threat, prayer, promise, action, resolve. Berryman always insisted on their unity – 'The Care & Feeding of Long Poems' was his special study – but that no longer seems a plausible or even an important claim, if it ever did. (Nor, analogously, does the siting or defining of Henry: he may not *be* Berryman, but he shares many of the trials and tribulations of the twentieth-century American poet.) Reading through all of them is like remaining in your seat while the lights go up and down on 385 phantasmagoric sketches, all with their own scenery and many of the best ones with more than one character. I think Harry Thomas is right when he finds that 'the impression made by reading several songs individually [...] is greater than that made by reading the work from end to end'. In that spirit, I offer my selection of just under one-sixth of them.

With the late poems, it is their plainness and cunning that touch me. The serpentine of 'Olympus', the circularity of 'Dante's Tomb', the occasional sumptuousness of the 'Addresses to the Lord'. In 'First Night at Sea' I value the revisiting of Dream Song #283; in 'He Resigns' the tragic echo of Sonnet #29; in 'Old Man Goes South Again Alone' the sound – down, or up to the title – of late Stevens.

MICHAEL HOFMANN

JOHN BERRYMAN

from *The Dispossessed*

A Professor's Song

(... rabid or dog-dull.) Let me tell you how
The Eighteenth Century couplet ended. Now
Tell me. Troll me the sources of that Song –
Assigned last week – by Blake. Come, come along,
Gentlemen. (Fidget and huddle, do. Squint soon.)
I want to end these fellows all by noon.

'That deep romantic chasm' – an early use;
The word is from the French, by our abuse
Fished out a bit. (Red all your eyes. O when?)
'A poet is a man speaking to men':
But I am then a poet, am I not? –
Ha ha. The radiator, please. Well, what?

Alive now – no – Blake would have written prose,
But movement following movement crisply flows,
So much the better, better the much so,
As burbleth Mozart. Twelve. The class can go.
Until I meet you, then, in Upper Hell
Convulsed, foaming immortal blood: farewell.

from *Berryman's Ssonnets*

[1]

I wished; all the mild days of middle March
This special year, your blond good-nature might
(Lady) admit – kicking abruptly tight
With will and affection down your breast like starch –
Me to your story, in Spring, and stretch, and arch.
But who not flanks the wells of uncanny light
Sudden in bright sand towering? A bone sunned white.
Considering travellers bypass these and parch.

This came to less yes than an ice cream cone
Let stand .. though still my sense of it is brisk:
Blond silky cream, sweet cold, aches: a door shut.
Errors of order! Luck lies with the bone,
Who rushed (and rests) to meet your small mouth, risk
Your teeth irregular and passionate.

[9]

Great citadels whereon the gold sun falls
Miss you O Lise sequestered to the West
Which wears you Mayday lily at its breast,
Part and not part, proper to balls and brawls,
Plains, cities, or the yellow shore, not false
Anywhere, free, native and Danishest
Profane and elegant flower, – whom suggest
Frail and not frail, blond rocks and madrigals.

Once in the car (cave of our radical love)
Your darker hair I saw than golden hair
Above your thighs whiter than white-gold hair,
And where the dashboard lit faintly your least
Enlarged scene, O the midnight bloomed .. the East
Less gorgeous, wearing you like a long white glove!

[11]

I expect you from the North. The path winds in
Between the honeysuckle and the pines, among
Poison ivy and small flowerless shrubs,
Across the red-brown needle-bed. I sit
Or smoking pace. A moment since, at six,
Mist wrapped the knoll, but now birds like a gong
Beat, greet the white-gold level shine. Wide-flung
On a thousand greens the late slight rain is gleaming.

A rabbit jumps a shrub. O my quick darling,
Lie torpid so? Cars from the highway whine,
Dawn's trunks against the sun are black. I shiver.
Your hair this fresh wind would – but I am starting.
To what end does this easy and crystal light
Dream on the flat leaves, emerald, and shimmer? ..

[13]

I lift – lift you five States away your glass,
Wide of this bar you never graced, where none
Ever I know came, where what work is done
Even by these men I know not, where a brass
Police-car sign peers in, wet strange cars pass,
Soiled hangs the rag of day out over this town,
A juke-box brains air where I drink alone,
The spruce barkeep sports a toupee alas –

My glass I lift at six o'clock, my darling,
As you plotted .. Chinese couples shift in bed,
We shared today not even filthy weather,
Beasts in the hills their tigerish love are snarling,
Suddenly they clash, I blow my short ash red,
Grey eyes light! and we have our drink together.

5

[23]

They may, because I would not cloy your ear –
If ever these songs by other ears are heard –
With 'love'; suppose I loved you not, but blurred
Lust with strange images, warm, not quite sincere,
To switch a bedroom black. O mutineer
With me against these empty captains! gird
Your scorn again above all at *this* word
Pompous and vague on the stump of his career.

Also I fox 'heart', striking a modern breast
Hollow as a drum, and 'beauty' I taboo;
I want a verse fresh as a bubble breaks,
As little false .. Blood of my sweet unrest
Runs all the same – I am in love with you –
Trapped in my rib-cage something throes and aches!

[29]

The cold rewards trail in, when the man is blind
They glitter round his tomb (no bivouac):
The Rue Fortunée is the Rue de Balzac,
The Bach-Gesellschaft girdles the world; unsigned,
The treaty rages freeing him to wind
Mankind about an icy finger. Pack
His laurel in, startle him with gimcrack
Recognition. – But O do not remind
Of the hours of morning this indifferent man
When alone in a summery cloud he sweat and knew
She, she would not come, she would not come, now
Or all the lime-slow day .. Your artisan
And men's, I tarry alike for fame and you,
Not hoping, tame, tapping my warm blank brow.

[32]

How shall I sing, western & dry & thin,
You who for celebration should cause flow
The sensual fanfare of D'Annunzio,
Mozart's mischievous joy, the amaranthine
Mild quirks of Marvell, Villon sharp as tin
Solid as sword-death when the man blinks slow
And accordions into the form he'll know
Forever – voices can nearly make me sin
With envy, so they sound. You they saw not,
Natheless, alas, unto this epigone
Descends the dread labour, the Olympic hour –
When for the garden and the tape of what
We trust, one runs until lung into bone
Hardens, runs harder then .. lucky, a flower.

[36]

Keep your eyes open when you kiss: do: when
You kiss. All silly time else, close them to;
Unsleeping, I implore you (dear) pursue
In darkness me, as I do you again
Instantly we part .. only me both then
And when your fingers fall, let there be two
Only, 'in that dream-kingdom': I would have you
Me alone recognize your citizen.

Before who wanted eyes, making love, so?
I do now. However we are driven and hide,
What state we keep all other states condemn,
We see ourselves, we watch the solemn glow
Of empty courts we kiss in .. Open wide!
You do, you do, and I look into them.

[37]

Sigh as it ends .. I keep an eye on your
Amour with Scotch, – too *cher* to consummate;
Faster your disappearing beer than late-
ly mine; your naked passion for the floor;
Your hollow leg; your hanker for one more
Dark as the Sundam Trench; how you dilate
Upon psychotics of this class, collate
Stages, and .. how long since you, well, *forbore*.

Ah, but the high fire sings on to be fed
Whipping our darkness by the lifting sea
A while, O darling drinking like a clock.
The tide comes on: spare, Time, from what you spread
Her story, – tilting a frozen Daiquiri,
Blonde, barefoot, beautiful,
        flat on the bare floor rivetted to Bach.

[64]

The dew is drying fast, a last drop glistens
White on a damaged leaf not far from me.
A pine-cone calmed here in a red-brown sea
Collects its straying forces now and listens:
A veery calls; south, a slow whistle loosens
My lone control. The flat sun finally
Flaws through the evergreen grove, and can be he –
If Lise comes – our renewed love lights and christens.

Tarry today? .. weeks the abandoned knoll
And I have waited. The needles are soft .. feel.
The village bell, or the college, tells me seven.
Much longer not sustains – will it again? –
Castaway time I scrabble tooth and nail,
I crush a cigarette black, and go down.

Swarthy when young; who took the tonsure; sign,
His coronation, wangled, his name re-said
For euphony; off to courts fluttered, and fled;
Professorships refused; upon one line
Worked years; and then that genial concubine.
Seventy springs he read, and wrote, and read.
On the day of the year his people found him dead
I read his story. Anew I studied mine.

Also there was Laura and three-seventeen
Sonnets to something like her .. twenty-one years ..
He never touched her. Swirl our crimes and crimes.
Gold-haired (too), dark-eyed, ignorant of rimes
Was she? Virtuous? The old brume seldom clears.
– Two guilty and crepe-yellow months
    Lise! be our surviving actual scene.

Fall and rise of her midriff bells. I watch.
Blue knee-long shorts, striped light shirt. Bright between
Copt hills of the cushion a lazy green
Her sun-incomparable face I watch.
A darkness dreams adown her softest crotch,
A hand dreams on her breast, two fingers lean,
The ring shows like a wound. Her hair swirls clean
Alone in the vague room's morning-after botch.

Endymion's Glaucus through a thousand years
Collected the bodies of lovers lost, until
His own beloved's body rustled and sighed ..
So I would, O to spring – blotting her fears,
The others in this house, the house, road, hill –
As once she up the stair sprang to me, lips wide!

[80]

Infallible symbolist! – Tanker driven ashore,
An oil-ship by a tropical hurricane
Wrecked on a Delaware beach, the postcard's scene;
On the reverse, words without signature:
Je m'en fiche du monde sans toi – in your
Hand for years busy in the liquid main
To tank you on – your Tulsa father's vein,
Oil. All the worked and wind-slapt waters roar.

O my dear I am sorry, sorry, and glad! and glad
To trope you helpless, there, and needing me,
Where the dangerous land meets the disordered sea ..
Rich on the edge we wait our salvage, sad
And joyous, nervous, that the hired men come
Whom we require, to split us painfully home.

[101]

Because I'd seen you not believe your lover,
Because you scouted cries come from no cliff,
Because to supplications you were stiff
As Ciro, O as Nero to discover
Slow how your subject loved you, I would hover
Between the slave and rebel – till this life
Arrives: '... was astonished as I would be if
I leaned against a house and the house fell over ...'

Well, it fell over, over: trust him now:
A stronger house than looked – *you leaned*, and crash,
My walls and ceiling were to be walked on. –
The same thing happened once in Chaplin, how
He solved it now I lose. – Walk on the trash ..
Walk softly, triste, – little is really gone.

[106]

Began with swirling, blind, unstilled oh still, –
The tide had set in toward the western door
And I was working with the tide, I bore
My panful of reflexion firm, until
A voice arrested me, – body, and will,
And panful, wheeled and spilt, tempted nerves tore,
And all uncome time blackened like the core
Of an apple on through man's heart moving still ..

At nine o'clock and thirty Thursday night,
In Nineteen XXXX, February
Twice-ten-day, by a doorway in McIntosh,
So quietly neither the rip's cold slosh
Nor the meshing of great wheels warned me, unwary,
An enigmatic girl smiled out my sight.

[107]

Darling I wait O in my upstairs box
O for your footfall, O for your footfáll
in the extreme heat – I don't mind at all,
it's silence has me and the no of clocks
keeping us isolated longer: rocks
did the first martyr and will do to stall
our enemies, I'll get up on the roof of the hall
and heave freely. The University of Soft Knocks

will headlines in the *Times* make: Fellow goes mad,
crowd panics, rhododendrons injured. Slow
will flow the obituaries while the facts get straight,
almost straight. He was in love and he was had.
That was it: he should have stuck to his own mate,
before he went a-conning across the sea-O.

[108]

I owe you, do I not, a roofer: though
My sister-*in*-law and her nephews stayed,
Not I stayed. O kind sister-outlaw, laid
Far off and legally four weeks, stoop low,
For my true thanks are fugitive also
Only to you; – stop off your cant, you jade,
Bend down, – *I* have not ever disobeyed
You; and you will hear what it is I owe.

I owe you thanks for evenings in your house
When .. neither here, nor there, nowhere, were you,
Nights like long knives; .. *two* letters! .. life like a mouse
Cheeseless, but trapt. Another debit to
Your kinder husband. From the country of Choice
Another province chopt, – and they were few.

[109]

Ménage à trois, like Tristan's, – difficult! ..
The convalescent Count; his mistress; fast
The wiry wild arthritic young fantast
In love with her, his genius occult,
His weakness blazing, ugly, an insult
A salutation; in his yacht they assed
Up and down the whole coast six months .. last
It couldn't: .. the pair to Paris. Chaos, result.

Well – but four worse! .. all four, marvellous friends –
Some horse-shit here, eh? – You admitted it,
Come, you did once .. and we *are friends*, I say. –
'La Cuchiani aima Tristan, mais ...'
(The biographer says) *unscrupulous* a bit,
Or utterly ... There, of course, the resemblance ends.

12

[112]

I break my pace now for a sonic boom,
the future's with & in us. I sit fired
but comes on strong with the fire fatigue: I'm tired.
'I'd drive my car across the living-room
if I could get it inside the house.' You loom
less, less than before when your voice choired
into my transept hear I now it, not expired
but half-dead with exhaustion, like Mr Bloom.

Dazzle, before I abandon you, my eyes,
my eyes which I need for journeys difficult
in which case it may be said that I survive you.
Your voice continues, with its lows & highs,
and I am a willing accomplice in the cult
and every word that I   have gasped of you is true.

[114]

You come blonde visiting through the black air
knocking on my hinged lawn-level window
and you will come for years, above, below,
& through to interrupt my study where
I'm sweating it out like asterisks: so there, –
you are the text, my work's broken down so
I found, after my grandmother died, slow,
and I had flown far South to her funeral spare

but crowded with relations, I found her last
letter unopened, much less answered: shame
overcame me so far I paused & cried
in my underground study, for all the past
undone & never again to walk tall, lame
at the mercy of your presence to abide.

All we were going strong last night this time,
the *mots* were flying & the frozen daiquiris
were downing, supine on the floor lay Lise
listening to Schubert grievous & sublime,
my head was frantic with a following rime:
it was a good evening, an evening to please,
I kissed her in the kitchen – ecstasies –
among so much good we tamped down the crime.

The weather's changing. This morning was cold,
as I made for the grove, without expectation,
some hundred Sonnets in my pocket, old,
to read her if she came. Presently the sun
yellowed the pines & my lady came not
in blue jeans & a sweater. I sat down & wrote.

from *Homage to Mistress Bradstreet*

[17]

The winters close, Springs open, no child stirs
under my withering heart, O seasoned heart
God grudged his aid.
All things else soil like a shirt.
Simon is much away. My executive stales.
The town came through for the cartway by the pales,
but my patience is short.
I revolt from, I am like, these savage foresters

[18]

whose passionless dicker in the shade, whose glance
impassive & scant, belie their murderous cries
when quarry seems to show.
Again I must have been wrong, twice.
Unwell in a new way. Can that begin?
God brandishes. O love, O I love. Kin,
gather. My world is strange
and merciful, ingrown months, blessing a swelling trance.

[19]

So squeezed, wince you I scream? I love you & hate
off with you. Ages! *Useless.* Below my waist
he has me in Hell's vise.
Stalling. He let go. Come back: brace
me somewhere. No. No. Yes! everything down
hardens I press with horrible joy down
my back cracks like a wrist
shame I am voiding oh behind it is too late

hide me forever I work thrust I must free
now I all muscles & bones concentrate
what is living from dying?
Simon I must leave you so untidy
Monster you are killing me Be sure
I'll have you later Women do endure
I can *can* no longer
and it passes the wretched trap whelming and I am me

drencht & powerful, I did it with my body!
One proud tug greens Heaven. Marvellous,
unforbidding Majesty.
Swell, imperious bells. I fly.
Mountainous, woman not breaks and will bend:
sways God nearby: anguish comes to an end.
Blossomed Sarah, and I
blossom. Is that thing alive? I hear a famisht howl.

Beloved household, I am Simon's wife,
and the mother of Samuel – whom greedy yet I miss
out of his kicking place.
More in some ways I feel at a loss,
freer. Cantabanks & mummers, nears
longing for you. Our chopping scores my ears,
our costume bores my eyes.
St. George to the good sword, rise! chop-logic's rife

& fever & Satan & Satan's ancient fere.
Pioneering is not feeling well,
not Indians, beasts.

Not all their riddling can forestall
one leaving. Sam, your uncle has had to
go fróm us to live with God. 'Then Aunt went too?'
Dear, she does wait still.
Stricken: 'Oh. Then he takes   us one by one.' My dear.

from *His Thought Made Pockets & the Plane Bucket*

Venice, 182–

White & blue my breathing lady leans
across me in the first light, so we kiss.
The corners of her eyes are white. I miss,
renew. She means
to smother me thro' years of this.

Hell chill young widows in the heel of night –
perduring loves, melody's thrusting, press
flush with the soft skin, whence they sprung! back. Less
ecstasy might
save us for speech & politeness.

I hear her howl now, and I slam my eyes
against the glowing face. Foul morning-cheese
stands fair compared to love. On waspish knees
our pasts surprise
and plead us livid. Now she frees

a heavy lock was pulling .. I kiss it,
lifting my hopeless lids – and all trace
of passion's vanisht from her eyes & face,
the lip I bit
is bluer, a blackhead at the base

of her smooth nose looks sullenly at me,
we look at each other in entire despair,
her eyes are swimming by mine, and I swear
sobbing quickly
we áre in love. The light hurts. 'There …'

from *Dream Songs*

1

Huffy Henry hid   the day,
unappeasable Henry sulked.
I see his point, – a trying to put things over.
It was the thought that they thought
they could *do* it made Henry wicked & away.
But he should have come out and talked.

All the world like a woolen lover
once did seem on Henry's side.
Then came a departure.
Thereafter nothing fell out as it might or ought.
I don't see how Henry, pried
open for all the world to see, survived.

What he has now to say is a long
wonder the world can bear & be.
Once in a sycamore I was glad
all at the top, and I sang.
Hard on the land wears the strong sea
and empty grows every bed.

3

A Stimulant for an Old Beast

Acacia, burnt myrrh, velvet, pricky stings.
– I'm not so young but not so very old,
said screwed-up lovely 23.
A final sense of being right out in the cold,
unkissed.
(– My psychiatrist can lick your psychiatrist.) Women get
    under things.

All these old criminals sooner or later
have had it. I've been reading old journals.
Gottwald & Co., out of business now.
Thick chests quit. Double agent, Joe.
She holds her breath like a seal
and is whiter & smoother.

Rilke was a *jerk*.
I admit his griefs & music
& titled spelled all-disappointed ladies.
A threshold worse than the circles
where the vile settle & lurk,
Rilke's. As I said, –

4

Filling her compact & delicious body
with chicken páprika, she glanced at me
twice.
Fainting with interest, I hungered back
and only the fact of her husband & four other people
kept me from springing on her

or falling at her little feet and crying
'You are the hottest one for years of night
Henry's dazed eyes
have enjoyed, Brilliance.' I advanced upon
(despairing) my spumoni. – Sir Bones: is stuffed,
de world, wif feeding girls.

– Black hair, complexion Latin, jewelled eyes
downcast ... The slob beside her   feasts ... What wonders is
she sitting on, over there?
The restaurant buzzes. She might as well be on Mars.
Where did it all go wrong? There ought to be a law against
   Henry.
– Mr Bones: there is.

Life, friends, is boring. We must not say so.
After all, the sky flashes, the great sea yearns,
we ourselves flash and yearn,
and moreover my mother told me as a boy
(repeatingly) 'Ever to confess you're bored
means you have no

Inner Resources.' I conclude now I have no
inner resources, because I am heavy bored.
Peoples bore me,
literature bores me, especially great literature,
Henry bores me, with his plights & gripes
as bad as achilles,

who loves people and valiant art, which bores me.
And the tranquil hills, & gin, look like a drag
and somehow a dog
has taken itself & its tail considerably away
into mountains or sea or sky, leaving
behind: me, wag.

Henry's pelt was put on sundry walls
where it did much resemble Henry and
them persons was delighted.
Especially his long & glowing tail
by all them was admired, and visitors.
They whistled: This is *it*!

Golden, whilst your frozen daiquiris
whir at midnight, gleams on you his fur
& silky & black.
Mission accomplished, pal.
My molten yellow & moonless bag,
drained, hangs at rest.

Collect in the cold depths barracuda. Ay,
in Sealdah Station some possessionless
children survive to die.
The Chinese communes hum. Two daiquiris
withdrew into a corner of the gorgeous room
and one told the other a lie.

A Strut for Roethke

Westward, hit a low note, for a roarer lost
across the Sound but north from Bremerton,
hit a way down note.
And never cadenza again of flowers, or cost.
Him who could really do that cleared his throat
& staggered on.

The bluebells, pool-shallows, saluted his over-needs,
while the clouds growled, heh-heh, & snapped, & crashed.

No stunt he'll ever unflinch once more will fail
(O lucky fellow, eh Bones?) – drifted off upstairs,
downstairs, somewheres.
No more daily, trying to hit the head on the nail:
thirstless: without a think in his head:
back from wherever, with it said.

Hit a high long note, for a lover found
needing a lower into friendlier ground
to bug among worms no more
around um jungles where ah blurt 'What for?'
Weeds, too, he favoured as   most men don't favour men.
The Garden Master's gone.

Here, whence
all have departed or will do, here airless, where
that witchy ball
wanted, fought toward, dreamed of, all a green living
drops limply into one's hands
without pleasure or interest

Figurez-vous, a time swarms when the word
'happy' sheds its whole meaning, like to come and
like for memory too
That morning arrived to Henry as well a great cheque
eaten out already by the Government & State &
other strange matters

Gentle friendly Henry Pussy-cat
smiled into his mirror, a murderer's
(at Stillwater), at himself alone
and said across a plink to that desolate fellow
said a little hail & buck-you-up
upon his triumph

The Lay of Ike

This is the lay of Ike.
Here's to the glory of the Great White – awk –
who has been running – er – er – things in recent – ech –
in the United – If your screen is black,
ladies & gentlemen, we – I like –
at the Point he was already terrific – sick

to a second term, having done no wrong –
no right – no right – having let the Army – bang –
defend itself from Joe, let venom' Strauss
bile Oppenheimer out of use – use Robb,
who'll later fend for Goldfine – Breaking no laws,
he lay in the White House – sob!! –

who never understood his own strategy – whee –
so Monty's memoirs – nor any strategy,
wanting the ball bulled thro' all parts of the line
at once – proving, by his refusal to take Berlin,
he misread even Clauswitz – wide empty grin
that never lost a vote (O Adlai mine).

Oh servant Henry lectured till
the crows commenced and then
he bulbed his voice & lectured on some more.
This happened again & again, like war, –
the Indian p.a.'s, such as they were,
a weapon on his side, for the birds.

Vexations held a field-monsoon.
He was Introduced, and then he was Summed-up.
He was put questions on race bigotry;
he put no questions on race bigotry
constantly.
The mad sun rose though on the ghats
  & the saddhu in maha mudra, the great River,

and Henry was happy & beside him with excitement.
Beside himself, his possibilities;
salaaming hours of a half-blind morning
while the rainy lepers salaamed back,
smiles & a passion of their & his eyes flew
in feelings not ever accorded solely to oneself.

The glories of the world struck me, made me aria, once.
– What happen then, Mr Bones?
if be you cares to say.
– Henry. Henry became interested in women's bodies,
his loins were & were the   scene of stupendous achievement.
Stupor. Knees, dear. Pray.

All the knobs & softnesses of, my God,
the ducking & trouble it swarm on Henry,
at one time.
– What happen then, Mr Bones?
you seems excited-like.
 – Fell Henry back into   the original crime: art, rime

besides a sense of others, my God, my God,
and a jealousy for the honour (alive) of his country,
what can get more odd?
and discontent with the thriving gangs & pride.
 – What happen then, Mr Bones?
 – I had a most marvellous   piece of luck. I died.

Snow Line

It was wet & white & swift and where I am
we don't know. It was dark and then
it isn't.
I wish the barker would come. There seems to be to eat
nothing. I am unusually tired.
I'm alone too.

If only the strange one with so few legs would come,
I'd say my prayers out of my mouth, as usual.
Where are his notes I loved?
There may be horribles; it's hard to tell.
The barker nips me but somehow I feel
he too is on my side.

I'm too alone. I see no end. If we could all
run, even that would be better. I am hungry.
The sun is not hot.
It's not a good position I am in.
If I had to do the whole thing over again
I wouldn't.

There sat down, once, a thing on Henry's heart
só heavy, if he had a hundred years
& more, & weeping, sleepless, in all them time
Henry could not make good.
Starts again always in Henry's ears
the little cough somewhere, an odour, a chime.

And there is another thing he has in mind
like a grave Sienese face a thousand years
would fail to blur the still profiled reproach of. Ghastly,
with open eyes, he attends, blind.
All the bells say: too late. This is not for tears;
thinking.

But never did Henry, as he thought he did,
end anyone and hacks her body up
and hide the pieces, where they may be found.
He knows: he went over everyone, & nobody's missing.
Often he reckons, in the dawn, them up.
Nobody is ever missing.

Three around the Old Gentleman

His malice was a pimple down his good
big face, with its sly eyes. I must be sorry
Mr Frost has left:
I like it so less I don't understood –
he couldn't hear or see well – all we sift –
but this is a *bad* story.

He had fine stories and was another man
in private; difficult, always. Courteous,
on the whole, in private.
He apologize to Henry, off & on,
for two blue slanders; which was good of him.
I don't know how he made it.

Quickly, off stage with all but kindness, now.
I can't say what I have in mind. Bless Frost,
any odd god around.
Gentle his shift, I decussate & command,
stoic deity. For a while here we possessed
an unusual man.

I'm scared a lonely. Never see my son,
easy be not to see anyone,
combers out to sea
know they're goin somewhere but not me.
Got a little poison, got a little gun,
I'm scared a lonely.

I'm scared a only one thing, which is me,
from othering I don't take nothin, see,
for any hound dog's sake.
But this is where I livin, where I rake
my leaves and cop my promise, this' where we
cry oursel's awake.

Wishin was dyin but I gotta make
it all this way to that bed on these feet
where peoples said to meet.
Maybe but even if I see my son
forever never, get back on the take,
free, black & forty-one.

'Oyez, oyez!' The Man Who Did Not Deliver
is before you for his deliverance, my lords.
He stands, as charged
for This by banks, That cops, by lawyers, by
publishingers for Them. I doubt he'll make
old bones.

Be.
I warned him, of a summer night: consist,
consist. Ex-wives roar.
Further, the Crown holds that they spilt himself,
splitting his manward chances, to his shame,
my lords, & our horror.

Behind, oh worst lean backward them who bring
un-charges: hundreds & one, children,
the pillars & the sot.
Henry thought. It is so. I must sting.
Listen! the grave ground-rhythm of a gone
... makar? So what.

I am, outside. Incredible panic rules.
People are blowing and beating each other without mercy.
Drinks are boiling. Iced
drinks are boiling. The worse anyone feels, the worse
treated he is. Fools elect fools.
A harmless man at an intersection said, under his breath:
  'Christ!'

That word, so spoken, affected the vision
of, when they trod to work next day, shopkeepers
who went & were fitted for glasses.
Enjoyed they then an appearance of love & law.
Millenia whift & waft – one, one – er, er ...
Their glasses were taken from them, & they saw.

Man has undertaken the top job of all,
son fin. Good luck.
I myself walked at the funeral of tenderness.
Followed other deaths. Among the last,
like the memory of a lovely fuck,
was: *Do, ut des.*

That dark brown rabbit, lightness in his ears
& underneath, gladdened our afternoon
munching a crab-'.
That rabbit was a fraud, like a black bull
prudent I admired in Zaragoza, who
certainly was brave as a demon

but would not charge, being willing not to die.
The rabbit's case, a little different,
consisted in alert
& wily looks down the lawn, where nobody was,
with prickt ears, while rapt but chatting on the porch
we sat in view nearby.

Then went he mildly by, and around behind
my cabin, and when I followed, there he just sat.
Only at last
he turned down around, passing my wife at four feet
and hopped the whole lawn and made thro' the hedge for the
   big house.
 – Mr Bones, we all brutes & fools.

Bats have no bankers and they do not drink
and cannot be arrested and pay no tax
and, in general, bats have it made.
Henry for joining the human race is *bats*,
known to be so, by few them who think,
out of the cave.

Instead of the cave! ah lovely-chilly, dark,
ur-moist his cousins hang in hundreds or swerve
with personal radar,
crisisless, kid. Instead of the cave? I serve,
inside, my blind term. Filthy four-foot lights
reflect on the whites of our eyes.

He then salutes for sixty years of it
just now a one of valor and insights,
a theatrical man,
O scholar & Legionnaire who as quickly might
have killed as cast you. *Olè*. Stormed with years
he tranquil commands and appears.

68

I heard, could be, a Hey there from the wing,
and I went on: Miss Bessie soundin good
that one, that night of all,
I feelin fair mysef, taxes & things
seem to be back in line, like everybody should
and nobody in the snow on call

so, as I say, the house is givin hell
to *Yellow Dog*, I blowin like it too
and Bessie always do
when she make a very big sound – after, well,
no sound – I see she totterin – I cross which stage
even at Henry's age

in 2–3 seconds: then we wait and see.
I hear strange horns, Pinetop he hit some chords,
Charlie start *Empty Bed*,
they all come hangin Christmas on some tree
after trees thrown out – sick-house's white birds',
black to the birds instead.

Love her he doesn't but the thought he puts
into that young woman
would launch a national product
complete with TV spots & skywriting
outlets in Bonn & Tokyo
I mean it

Let it be known that nine words have not passed
between herself and Henry;
looks, smiles.
God help Henry, who deserves it all
every least part of that infernal & unconscious
woman, and the pain.

I feel as if, unique, she ... Biddable?
Fates, conspire.
– Mr Bones, *please.*
– Vouchsafe me, Sleepless One,
a personal experience of the body of Mrs Boogry
before I pass from lust!

Henry hates the world. What the world to Henry
did will not bear thought.
Feeling no pain,
Henry stabbed his arm and wrote a letter
explaining how bad it had been
in this world.

Old yellow, in a gown
might have made a difference, 'these lower beauties',
and chartreuse could have mattered

'Kyoto, Toledo,
Benares – the holy cities –
and Cambridge shimmering do not make up
for, well, the horror of unlove,
nor south from Paris driving in the Spring
to Siena and on ...'

Pulling together Henry, somber Henry
woofed at things.
Spry disappointments of men
and vicing adorable children
miserable women, Henry mastered, Henry
tasting all the secret bits of life.

75

Turning it over, considering, like a madman
Henry put forth a book.
No harm resulted from this.
Neither the menstruating   stars (nor man) was moved
at once.
Bare dogs drew closer for a second look

and performed their friendly operations there.
Refreshed, the bark rejoiced.
Seasons went and came.
Leaves fell, but only a few.
Something remarkable about this
unshedding bulky bole-proud blue-green moist

thing made by savage & thoughtful
surviving Henry
began to strike the passers from despair
so that sore on their shoulders old men hoisted
six-foot sons and polished women called
small girls to dream awhile toward the flashing & bursting tree!

Henry's Confession

Nothin very bad happen to me lately.
How you explain that? – I explain that, Mr Bones,
terms o' your bafflin odd sobriety.
Sober as man can get, no girls, no telephones,
what could happen bad to Mr Bones?
– *If* life is a handkerchief sandwich,

in a modesty of death I join my father
who dared so long agone leave me.
A bullet on a concrete stoop
close by a smothering southern sea
spreadeagled on an island, by my knee.
 – You is from hunger, Mr Bones,

I offers you this handkerchief, now set
your left foot by my right foot,
shoulder to shoulder, all that jazz,
arm in arm, by the beautiful sea,
hum a little, Mr Bones.
– I saw nobody coming, so I went instead.

Seedy Henry rose up shy in de world
& shaved & swung his barbells, duded Henry up
and p.a.'d poor thousands of persons on topics of grand
moment to Henry, ah to those less & none.
Wif a book of his in either hand
he is stript down to move on.

– Come away, Mr Bones.

– Henry is tired of the winter,
& haircuts, & a squeamish comfy   ruin-prone proud national
    mind,   & Spring (in the city so called).
Henry likes Fall.
Hé would be prepared to líve in a world of Fáll
for ever, impenitent Henry.
But the snows and summers grieve & dream;

thése fierce & airy occupations, and love,
raved away so many of Henry's years
it is a wonder that, with in each hand
one of his own mad books and all,
ancient fires for eyes, his head full
& his heart full, he's making ready to move on.

Op. posth. no. 3

It's buried at a distance, on my insistence, buried.
Weather's severe there, which it will not mind.
I miss it.
O happies before & during & between the times it got married.
I hate the love of leaving it behind,
deteriorating & hopeless that.

The great Uh climbed above me, far above me,
doing the north face, or behind it. Does He love me?
over, & flout.
Goodness is bits of outer God. The house-guest
(slimmed-down) with one eye open & one breast
out.

Slimmed-down from by-blow; adoptive-up; was white.
A daughter of a friend. His soul is a sight.
– Mr Bones, what's all about?
Girl have a little: what be wrong with *that?*
Yóu free? – Down some many did descend
from the abominable & semi-mortal Cat.

Op. posth. no. 4

He loom' so cagey he say 'Leema beans'
and measured his intake to the atmosphere
of that fairly stable country.
His ear hurt. Left. The rock-cliffs, a mite sheer
at his age, in these places.
Scrubbing out his fear, –

the knowledge that they will take off your hands,
both hands; as well as your both feet, & likewise
both eyes,
might be discouraging to a bloody hero
Also you stifle, like you can't draw breath.
But this is death –

which in some vain strive many to avoid,
many. It's on its way, where you drop at
who stood up, scrunch down small.
It wasn't so much after all to lose, was, Boyd?
A body. – But, Mr Bones, you needed that.
Now I put on my tall hat.

Op. posth. no. 5

Maskt as honours, insult like behaving
missiles homes. I bow, & grunt 'Thank you.
I'm glad you could come
so late.' All loves are gratified. I'm having
to screw a little thing I have to screw.
Good nature is over.

Herewith ill-wishes. From a cozy grave
rainbow I scornful laughings. Do not do,
Father, me down.
Let's shuck an obligation. O I have
done. Is the inner-coffin burning blue
or did Jehovah frown?

Jehovah. Period. Yahweh. Period. God.
It is marvellous that views so differay
(Father is a Jesuit)
can love so well each other. We was had.
O visit in my last tomb me. – Perché?
– Is a *nice* pit.

Op. posth. no. 12

In a blue series towards his sleepy eyes
they slid like wonder, women tall & small,
of every shape & size,
in many languages to lisp 'We do'
to Henry almost waking. What is the night at all,
his closed eyes beckon you.

In the Marriage of the Dead, a new routine,
he gasped his crowded vows past lids shut tight
and a-many rings fumbled on.
His coffin like Grand Central to the brim
filled up & emptied with the lapse of light.
Which one will waken him?

O she must startle like a fallen gown,
content with speech like an old sacrament
in deaf ears lying down,
blazing through darkness till he feels the cold
& blindness of his hopeless tenement
while his black arms unfold.

Op. posth. no. 13

In the night-reaches dreamed he of better graces,
of liberations, and beloved faces,
such as now ere dawn he sings.
It would not be easy, accustomed to these things,
to give up the old world, but he could try;
let it all rest, have a good cry.

Let Randall rest, whom your self-torturing
cannot restore one instant's good to, rest:
he's left us now.
The panic died and in the panic's dying
so did my old friend. I am headed west
also, also, somehow.

In the chambers of the end we'll meet again
I will say Randall, he'll say Pussycat
and all will be as before
whenas we sought, among the beloved faces,
eminence and were dissatisfied with that
and needed more.

Op. posth. no. 14

Noises from underground made gibber some,
others collected & dug Henry up
saying 'You *are* a sight.'
Chilly, he muttered for a double rum
waving the mikes away, putting a stop
to rumours, pushing his fright

off with the now accumulated taxes
accustomed in his way to solitude
and no bills.
Wives came forward, claiming a new Axis,
fearful for their insurance, though, now, glued
to disencumbered Henry's many ills.

A fortnight later, sense a single man
upon the trampled scene at 2 a.m.
insomnia-plagued, with a shovel
digging like mad, Lazarus with a plan
to get his own back, a plan, a stratagem
no newsman will unravel.

96

Under the table, no. That last was stunning,
that flagon had breasts. Some men grow down cursed.
Why drink so, two days running?
two months, O seasons, years, two decades running?
I answer (smiles) my question on the cuff:
Man, I been thirsty.

The brake is incomplete but white costumes
threaten his rum, his cointreau, gin-&-sherry,
his bourbon, bugs um all.
His go-out privilege led to odd red times,
since even or especially in hospital things get hairy.
He makes it back without falling.

He sleep up a short storm.
He wolf his meals, lamb-warm.

Their packs bump on their '-blades, tan canteens swing,
for them this day my dawn's old, Saturday's IT,
through town toward a Scout hike.
For him too, up since two, out for a sit
now in the emptiest freshest park, one sober fling
before correspondence & breakfast.

Three 'coons come at his garbage. He be cross,
I figuring porcupine & took Sir poker
unbarring Mr door,
& then screen door. Ah, but the little 'coon,
hardly a foot (not counting tail) got in with
two more at the porch-edge

and they swirled, before some two swerve off
this side of crab tree, and my dear friend held
with the torch in his tiny eyes
two feet off, banded, but then he gave &
shot away too. They were all the same size,
maybe they were brothers,

it seems, and is, clear to me we are brothers.
I wish the rabbit & the 'coons could be friends,
I'm sorry about the poker
but I'm too busy now for nipping or quills
I've given up literature & taken down pills,
and that rabbit doesn't trust me

108

Sixteen below. Our cars like stranded hulls
litter all day our little Avenue.
It *was* 28 below.
No one goes anywhere. Fabulous calls
to duty clank. Icy dungeons, though,
have much to mention to you.

At Harvard & Yale must Pussy-cat be heard
in the dead of winter when we must be sad
and feel by the weather had.
Chrysanthemums crest, far away, in the Emperor's garden
and, whenever we are, we must beg always pardon
Pardon was the word.

Pardon was the only word, in ferocious cold
like Asiatic prisons, where we live
and strive and strive to forgive.
Melted my honey, summers ago. I told
her true & summer things. She leaned an ear
in my direction, here.

Fresh-shaven, past months & a picture in New York
of Beard Two, I did have Three took off. Well . .
Shadow & act, shadow & act,
Better get white or you' get whacked,
or keep so-called *black*
& raise new hell.

I've had enough of this dying.
You've done me a dozen goodnesses; get well.
Fight again for our own.
Henry felt baffled, in the middle of the thing.
He spent his whole time in Ireland on the Book of Kells,
the jackass, made of bone.

No tremor, no perspire: Heaven is here
now, in Minneapolis.
It's easier to vomit than it was,
beardless.
There's always the cruelty of scholarship.
I once was a slip.

Bards freezing, naked, up to the neck in water,
wholly in dark, time limited, different from
initiations now:
the class in writing, clothed & dry & light,
unlimited time, till *Poetry* takes some,
nobody reads them though,

no trumpets, no solemn instauration, no change;
no commissions, ladies high in soulful praise
(pal) none,
costumes as usual, turtleneck sweaters, loafers,
in & among the busy Many who brays
art is if anything fun.

I say the subject was given as of old,
prescribed the technical treatment, tests really tests
were set by the masters & graded.
I say the paralyzed fear lest one's not one
is back with us forever, worsts & bests
spring for the public, faded.

Sick at 6 & sick again at 9
was Henry's gloomy Monday morning oh.
Still he had to lecture.
They waited, his little children, for stricken Henry
to rise up yet once more again and come oh.
They figured he was a fixture,

nuts to their bolts, keys to their bloody locks.
One day the whole affair will fall apart
with a rustle of fire,
a wrestle of undoing, as of tossed clocks,
and somewhere not far off a broken heart
for hire.

He had smoked a pack of cigarettes by 10
& was ready to go. Peace to his ashes then,
poor Henry,
with all this gas & shit blowing through it
four times in 2 hours, his tail ached.
He arose, benign, & performed.

The animal moment, when   he sorted out her tail
in a rump session with the vivid hostess
whose guests had finally gone,
was stronger, though so limited, though failed
all normal impulse before her interdiction, yes,
and Henry gave in.

I'd like to have your baby, but, she moaned,
I'm married. Henry muttered to himself
So am I and was glad
to keep chaste. If this lady he had had
scarcely could he have have ever forgiven himself
and how would he have atoned?

– Mr Bones, you strong on moral these days, hey?
It's good to be faithful but it ain't natural,
as you knows.
– I knew what I knew when I knew when I was astray,
all those bright painful years, forgiving all
but when Henry & his wives came to blows.

– That's enough of that, Mr Bones. *Some* lady you make.
Honour the burnt cork, be a vaudeville man,
I'll sing you now a song
the like of whích may bring your heart to break:
he's gone! and we don't know where. When he began
taking the pistol out & along,

you was just a little; but gross fears
accompanied us along the beaches, pal.
My mother was scared almost to death.
He was going to swim out, with me, forevers,
and a swimmer strong he was in the phosphorescent   Gulf,
but he decided on lead.

That mad drive wiped out my childhood. I put him down
while all the same on forty years I love him
stashed in Oklahoma
besides his brother Will. Bite the nerve of the town
for anyone so desperate. I repeat: I love him
until *I* fall into coma.

145

Also I love him: me he's done no wrong
for going on forty years – forgiveness time –
I touch now his despair,
he felt as bad as Whitman on his tower
but he did not swim out with me or my brother
as he threatened –

a powerful swimmer, to   take one of us along
as company in the defeat sublime,
freezing my helpless mother:
he only, very early in the morning,
rose with his gun and went outdoors by my window
and did what was needed.

I cannot read that wretched mind, so strong
& so undone. I've always tried. I – I'm
trying to forgive
whose frantic passage, when he could not live
an instant longer, in the summer dawn
left Henry to live on.

This world is gradually becoming a place
where I do not care to be any more. Can Delmore die?
I don't suppose
in all them years a day went ever by
without a loving thought for him. Welladay.
In the brightness of his promise,

unstained, I saw him thro' the mist of the actual
blazing with insight, warm with gossip
thro' all our Harvard years
when both of us were just becoming known
I got him out of a police-station once, in Washington, the
    world is *tref*
and grief too astray for tears.

I imagine you have heard the terrible news,
that Delmore Schwartz is dead, miserably & alone,
in New York: he sang me a song
'I am the Brooklyn poet Delmore Schwartz
Harms & the child I sing, two parents' torts'
when he was young & gift-strong.

He had followers but they could not find him;
friends but they could not find him. He hid his gift
in the center of Manhattan,
without a girl, in cheap hotels,
so disturbed on the street friends avoided him
Where did he come by his lift

which all we must or we would rapidly die:
did he remember the more beautiful & fresh poems
of early manhood now?
or did his subtle & strict standards allow
them nothing, baffled? What then did self-love show
of the weaker later, somehow?

I'd bleed to say his lovely work improved
but it is not so. He painfully removed
himself from the ordinary contacts
and shook with resentment. What final thought
solaced his fall to the hotel carpet, if any,
& the *New York Times*'s facts?

Bitter & bleary over Delmore's dying:
his death stopped clocks, let no activity
mar our hurrah of mourning,
let's all be Jews bereft, for he was one
He died too soon, he liked 'An Ancient to Ancients'
His death clouded the grove

I need to hurry this out before I forget
which I will never   He fell on the floor
outside a cheap hotel-room
my tearducts are worn out, the ambulance came
and there on the way he died
He was 'smart & kind,'

a child's epitaph. He had no children,
nobody to stand by in the awful years
of the failure of his administration
He was tortured, beyond what man might be
Sick & heartbroken Henry sank to his knees
Delmore is dead. His good body lay unclaimed
three days.

Flagrant his young male beauty, thick his mind
with lore and passionate, white his devotion
to Gertrude only,
but even that marriage fell on days were lonely
and ended, and the trouble with friends got into motion,
when Delmore undermined

his closest loves with merciless suspicion:
Dwight cheated him out of a house, Saul withheld money,
and then to cap it all,
Henry was not here in '57
during his troubles (Henry was in Asia),
accusations to appall

the Loyal forever, but the demands increast:
as I said to my house in Providence
at 8 a.m. in a Cambridge taxi,
which he had wait, later he telephoned
at midnight from New York, to bring my family
to New York, leaving my job.

All your bills will be paid, he added, tense.

I can't get him out of my mind, out of my mind,
Hé was out of his own mind for years,
in police stations & Bellevue.
He drove up to my house in Providence
ho ho at 8 a.m. in a Cambridge taxi
and told it to wait.

He walked my living-room, & did not want breakfast
or even coffee, or even even a drink.
He paced, I'd say Sit down,
it makes me nervous, for a moment he'd sit down,
then pace. After an hour or so *I* had a drink.
He took it back to Cambridge,

we never learnt why he came, or what he wanted.
His mission was obscure. His mission was real,
but obscure.
I remember his electrical insight as the young man,
his wit & passion, gift, the whole young man
alive with surplus love.

An orange moon upon a placid sea
glistened for criminal Henry's fiery arm
fractured in the humerus:
no joke to Henry, nothing humorous
about his broken, he loved emptily
the rest of his body, warm

but not too warm, like this delinquent member.
His fingers wiggle, wiggle too his toes
like a sound person's.
He found himself okay, save for dispersings
of pain across his gross shaft, hard as blows
that in deep woods fell timber.

O prostrate body, busy with your break,
false tissue forming, striving to recover,
when will you make do like the moon
cold on a placid sea, with three limbs, take
the other for a cruise, like an elderly lover
not expecting much.

– I can't read any more of this Rich Critical Prose,
he growled, broke wind, and scratched himself & left
that fragrant area.
When the mind dies it exudes rich critical prose,
especially about Henry, particularly in Spanish, and sends it to
   him
from Madrid, London, New York.

Now back on down, boys; don't expressed yourself,
begged for their own sake sympathetic Henry,
his spirit full with Mark Twain
and also his memory, lest they might strain
theirselves, to alter the best anecdote
that even he ever invented.

Let the mail demain contain no pro's or con's,
or photographs or prose or sharp translations.
Let one-armed Henry be.
A solitaire of English, free of dons
& journalists, keeping trying in one or two nations
to put his boat back to sea.

Go, ill-sped book, and whisper to her or
storm out the message for her only ear
that she is beautiful.
Mention sunsets, be not silent of her eyes
and mouth and other prospects, praise her size,
say her figure is full.

Say her small figure is heavenly & full,
so as stunned Henry yatters like a fool
& maketh little sense.
Say she is soft in speech, stately in walking,
modest at gatherings, and in every thing
declare her excellence.

Forget not, when the rest is wholly done
and all her splendours opened one by one
to add that she likes Henry,
for reasons unknown, and fate has bound them fast
one to another in linkages that last
and that are fair to see.

There is a kind of undetermined hair,
half-tan, to which he was entirely unable to fail to respond
in woman, a poisoned
reminiscence: a kiss, or so; there.
The lady is not pretty but has eyes,
and seems to be kind.

Convulsed with love, who cares? There is that hair
unbuttoned. Loves unbutton loves, we're bare,
somewhere in my mind.
When this occurs I begin to think in Spanish
when Miss Cienfuegos, who looked after me
& after me in Pasadena.

Murdered the ruses that would quack me clear
The orchard squeaks. I look less weird
without my beard
Cal has always manifested a most surprising affection
for Matthew Arnold, – who is not a rat but whom
I can quite take or leave.

Come & dance, Housman's hopeless heroine
bereft of all: I take you in me arms
burnt-cork:
your creator is studying his celestial sphere,
he never loved you, he never loved a woman
or a man, save one: he was a fork

saved by his double genius & certain emendations
All his long life, hopeless lads grew cold
He drew their death-masks
To listen to him, you'd think that growing old
at twenty-two was horrible, and the ordinary tasks
of people didn't exist.

He did his almost perfect best with what he had
Shades are sorrowing, as not called up
by in his genius him
Others are for his life-long omission glad
& published their works as soon as he came to a stop
& could not review them.

So Long? Stevens

He lifted up, among the actuaries,
a grandee crow. Ah ha & he crowed good.
That funny money-man.
Mutter we all must as well as we can.
He mutter spiffy. He make wonder Henry's
wits, though, with a odd

... something ... something ... not there in his flourishing art.
O veteran of death, you will not mind
a counter-mutter.
What was it missing, then, at the man's heart
so that he does not wound? It is our kind
to wound, as well as utter

a fact of happy world. That metaphysics
he hefted up until we could not breathe
the physics. *On our side*,
monotonous (or ever-fresh) – it sticks
in Henry's throat to judge – brilliant, he seethe;
better than us; less wide.

Shrouded the great stars, the great boat moves on.
A minimum of tremor in the bar.
Today was Children's Day
& the Little Twiss prinked out ah as a bunny
won or did not win – I forget – second prize:
I forget to say.

I forget the great ship steaming thro' the dark
I forget the souls *so* eager for their pain.
Two have just dropt in,
grand ships' officers, large heads & gold braid,
the authority of the bartender is dwarfed
I forget all the old

I seem to be Henry then at twenty-one
steaming the sea again   in another British boat
again, half mad with hope:
with my loved Basque friend I stroll the topmost deck
high in the windy night, in love with life
which has produced this wreck.

I broke a mirror, in which I figured you.
Henry did not lavish his hopes: he hoped to destroy
with this one act
the counter-forces against your art's design,
the burgeon of your heart. You have enemies,
my dear. It is a fact

that you have enemies: one word of praise
has grouped against you gangs against that word
of decent praise:
I urge you, with misgivings, on, these days,
the temperature of the end has not been taken,
so I have heard,

I trust your detestation of Carlyle
the evil way a genius can go.
I hope you hate Carlyle
& Emerson's insufferable essays,
wisdom in every line, while his wife cried upstairs,
disgusting Emerson & Rilke.

Like the sunburst up the white breast of a black-footed
   penguin
amid infinite quantities of gin
Henry perceived his subject.
It came nearer, like a guilty bystander,
stood close, leaving no room to ponder,
Mickey Mouse & The Tiger on the table.

Leaving the ends aft open, touch the means,
whereby we ripen. Touch by all means the means
whereby we come to life,
enduring the manner for the matter, ay
I sing quickly, offered Henry, I
sing more quickly.

I sing with infinite slowness finite pain
I have reached into the corner of my brain
to have it out.
I sat by fires when I was young, & now
I'm not I sit by fires again, although
I do it more slowly.

An Instructions to Critics

The women of Kilkenny weep when the team loses,
they don't see the match but they cry. Mad bettors everywhere,
the sign 'Turf Accountant',
men slipping in & out. People are all the same,
the seaman argued: Henry feels the Spanish & Irish
& Bengalis are thoroughly odd.

Americans, whom I prefer, are hopelessly normal.
The Japanese are barely comprehensible & formal,
formal Henry found.
We should have lowered the boom
on ourselves in our mother's womb,
dixit Henry's pal above ground.

My baby chatters. I feel the end is near
& strong of my large work, which will appear,
and baffle everybody.
They'll seek the strange soul, in rain & mist,
whereas they should recall the pretty cousins they kissed,
and stick with the sweet switch of the body.

Control it now, it can't do any good,
your grief for your great friend, killed on the day
he &   his wife&   three
were moving to a larger house across the street.
Our dead frisk us, & later they get better at it,
our wits are stung astray

till all that we can do is groan, bereft:
tears fail: and then we reckon what is left,
not what was lost.
I notice at this point a divided soul,
headed both fore & aft and guess which soul
will swamp & lose:

that hoping forward, brisk & vivid one
of which will nothing ever be heard again.
Advance into the past!
Henry made lists of his surviving friends
& of the vanished on their uncanny errands
and took a deep breath.

The only happy people in the world
are those who do not have   to write long poems:
muck, administration, toil:
the protototality of an absence of contact
in one's own generation, chiefly the old & the young
persisting with interest.

'The Care & Feeding of Long Poems' was Henry's title
for his next essay, which will come out when
he wants it to.
A Kennedy-sponsored bill for the protection
of poets from long poems   will benefit the culture
and do no harm to that kind Lady, Mrs Johnson.

He would have gone to the White House & consulted the
    President
during his 10 seconds in the receiving line
on the problems of long poems
Mr Johnson has never written one
but he seems a generous & able man
'Tetelestai' said St John.

Chilled in this Irish pub I wish my loves
well, well to strangers, well to all his friends,
seven or so in number,
I forgive my enemies, especially two,
races his heart, at so much magnanimity,
can it at all be true?

– Mr Bones, you on a trip outside yourself.
Has you seen a medicine man? You sound will-like,
a testament & such.
Is you going? – Oh, I suffer from a strike
& a strike & three balls: I stand up for much,
Wordsworth & that sort of thing.

The pitcher dreamed. He threw a hazy curve,
I took it in my stride & out I struck,
lonesome Henry.
These Songs are not meant to be understood, you understand.
They are only meant to terrify & comfort.
Lilac was found in his hand.

To the edge of Europe, the eighteenth edge,
the ancient edge, Henry sailed full of thought
and rich with high-wrought designs,
for a tranquil mind & to fulfil a pledge
he gave himself to end a labour, sought
but now his mind not finds

conformable itself to that forever
or any more of the stretch of Henry's years.
Strange & new outlines
blur the old project. Soon they dissever
the pen & the heart, the old heart with its fears
& the daughter for which it pines.

Fresh toils the lightning over the Liffey, wild
and the avenues, like Paris's, are rain
and Henry is here for a while
of many months, along with the squalls of a child,
thirty years later. I will not come again
or not come with this style.

from *Love and Fame*

Olympus

In my serpentine researches
I came on a book review in *Poetry*
which began, with sublime assurance,
a comprehensive air of majesty,

'The art of poetry
is amply distinguished from the manufacture of verse
by the animating presence in the poetry
of a fresh idiom: language

so twisted & posed in a form
that it not only expresses the matter in hand
but adds to the stock of available reality.'
I was never altogether the same man after *that*.

I found this new Law-giver all unknown
except in the back numbers of a Cambridge quarterly
Hound & Horn, just defunct.
I haunted on Sixth Avenue until

at 15¢ apiece or 25
I had all 28 numbers
& had fired my followers at Philolexian & Boar's Head
with the merits of this prophet.

My girls suffered during this month or so,
so did my seminars & lectures &
my poetry even. To be a *critic*, ah,
how deeper & more scientific,

I wrote & printed an essay on Yeats's plays
re-deploying all of Blackmur's key terms
& even his sentence-structure wherever I could.

When he answered by hand from Boston my nervous
    invitation

to come & be honoured at our annual Poetry Reading,
it must have been ten minutes before I could open the
    envelope.
I got *him* to review Tate's book of essays
& *Mark* to review *The Double Agent*. Olympus!

I have travelled in some high company since
less dizzily.
I have had some rare girls since but never one so philosophical
as that same Spring (my last Spring there) Jean Bennett.

First Night at Sea

I'm at a table with Canadians
He translates Villon. Villon! What Canadian
could English make of those abject bravura laments?
He says he'll give me a copy.

We walk the top deck in dark, Pedro Donga & I,
the Haitian proved a narcissist & we evade him.
He sings me a Basque folk-song, his father was Basque
passing through, his mother a Spanish lady

married, staying there. He ran away
at nine, with gypsies. At the University of Lyon
he assisted with experiments in resuscitation,
he says the Russians are ahead of us in this field.

He sang then for a night-club in Berlin
& got 50 sexual offers a week.
With Memel, the Belgian composer
he went to the Congo to collect tribal tunes.

I listened with three ears.

Now he lives a bachelor in Paris
thirty-three & he has to shave twice a day,
short, muscular.
We trade quotations of Lorca's ballads,

grave news of the Loyalists' fight to hold Madrid.
I have felt happy
before but not in the flying wind like this.
He says come see him at Christmas.

Of Suicide

Reflexions on suicide, & on my father, possess me.
I drink too much. My wife threatens separation.
She won't 'nurse' me. She feels 'inadequate'.
We don't mix together.

It's an hour later in the East.
I could call up Mother in Washington, D.C.
But could she help me?
And all this postal adulation & reproach?

A basis rock-like of love & friendship
for all this world-wide madness seems to be needed.
Epictetus is in some ways my favourite philosopher.
Happy men have died earlier.

I still plan to go to Mexico this summer.
The Olmec images! Chichén Itzá!
D. H. Lawrence has a wild dream of it.
Malcolm Lowry's book when it came out I taught to my
      precept at Princeton.

I don't entirely resign. I may teach the Third Gospel
this afternoon. I haven't made up my mind.
It seems to me sometimes that others have easier jobs
& do them worse.

Well, we must labour & dream. Gogol was impotent,
somebody in Pittsburgh told me.
I said: At what age? They couldn't answer.
That is a damned serious matter.

Rembrandt was sober. There we differ. Sober.
Terrors came on him. To us too they come.
Of suicide I continually think.
Apparently he didn't. I'll teach Luke.

Dante's Tomb

A tired banana & an empty mind
at 7 a.m. My world offends my eyes
bleary as an envelope cried-over
after the letter's lost.

In spite of it all, both it & me,
I'll chip away at the mystery.
There's a Toltec warrior in Minneapolis
with narrow eyes, reclining.

The head raised & facing you;
larger than life-size, in tan granite.
The cult perished.
The empty city welcomed the monkeys.

We don't *know*. Hundreds & hundreds of little poems
rolled up & tied with ribbons
over the virgin years, 'unwanted love'.
And Miss Bishop's friend has died,

and I will die and one day in Ravenna
I visited his tomb. A domed affair,
forbidding & tight shut.
'Dantis Poetae Sepulchrum.'

She said to me, half-strangled, 'Do that again.
And then do the other thing.'
Sunlight flooded the old room
& I was both sleepy & hungry.

from Eleven Addresses to the Lord

1

Master of beauty, craftsman of the snowflake,
inimitable contriver,
endower of Earth so gorgeous & different from the boring
    Moon,
thank you for such as it is my gift.

I have made up a morning prayer to you
containing with precision everything that most matters.
'According to Thy will' the thing begins.
It took me off & on two days. It does not aim at eloquence.

You have come to my rescue again & again
in my impassable, sometimes despairing years.
You have allowed my brilliant friends to destroy themselves
and I am still here, severely damaged, but functioning.

Unknowable, as I am unknown to my guinea pigs:
how can I 'love' you?
I only as far as gratitude & awe
confidently & absolutely go.

I have no idea whether we live again.
It doesn't seem likely
from either the scientific or the philosophical point of view
but certainly all things are possible to you,

and I believe as fixedly in the Resurrection-appearances to
    Peter and to Paul
  as I believe I sit in this blue chair.
Only that may have been a special case
to establish their initiatory faith.

Whatever your end may be, accept my amazement.
May I stand until death forever at attention

for any your least instruction or enlightenment.
I even feel sure you will assist me again, Master of insight &
    beauty.

6

Under new management, Your Majesty:
Thine. I have solo'd mine since childhood, since
my father's blow-it-all when I was twelve
blew out my most bright candle faith, and look at me.

I served at Mass six dawns a week from five,
adoring Father Boniface & you,
memorizing the Latin he explained.
Mostly we worked alone. One or two women.

Then my poor father frantic. Confusions & afflictions
followed my days. Wives left me.
Bankrupt I closed my doors. You pierced the roof
twice & again. Finally you opened my eyes.

My double nature fused in that point of time
three weeks ago day before yesterday.
Now, brooding thro' a history of the early Church,
I identify with everybody, even the heresiarchs.

9

Surprise me on some ordinary day
with a blessing gratuitous. Even I've done good
beyond their expectations. What count we then
upon Your bounty?

Interminable: an old theologian
asserts that even to say You exist is misleading.
Uh-huh. I buy that Second-century fellow.
I press his withered glorifying hand.

You certainly do not as I exist,
impersonating as well the meteorite
& flaring in your sun your waterfall
or blind in caves pallid fishes.

Bear in mind me, Who have forgotten nothing,
& Who continues. I may not foreknow
& fail much to remember. You sustain
imperial desuetudes, at the kerb a widow.

from *Delusions, etc*

In Memoriam (1914–1953)

I

Took my leave (last) five times before the end
and even past these precautions lost the end.
Oh, I *was* highlone in the corridor
    fifteen feet from his bed

where no other hovered, nurse or staff or friend,
and only the terrible breathing ever took place,
but trembling nearer after some small time
    I came on the tent collapsed

and silence – O unable to say when.
I stopped panicked a nurse, she a doctor
in twenty seconds, he pulled the plasticine,
    bent over, and shook his head at me.

Tubes all over, useless versus coma,
on the third day his principal physician
told me to pray he'd die, brain damage such.
    His bare stub feet stuck out.

II

So much for the age's prodigy, born one day
before I surfaced – when this fact emerged
Dylan grew stuffy and would puff all up
    rearing his head back and roar

'A little more – more – *respect* there, Berryman!'
Ah he had thát, – so far ahead of me,
I half-adored him for his intricate booms & indecent tales
    almost entirely untrue.

Scorn bottomless for elders: we were twenty-three
but Yeats I worshipped: he was amused by this,
all day the day set for my tea with the Great Man
    he plotted to turn me up drunk.

Downing me daily at shove-ha'penny
with *English* on the thing. C — would slump there
plump as a lump for hours, my word how that changed!
    Hard on her widowhood –

III

Apart a dozen years, sober in Seattle
'After many a summer' he intoned
putting out a fat hand. We shook hands.
    How very shook to see him.

His talk, one told me, clung latterly to Eden,
again & again of the Garden & the Garden's flowers,
not ever the Creator, only of that creation
    with a radiant will to go there.

I have sat hard for twenty years on this
mid potpals' yapping, and O I sit still still
though I quit crying that same afternoon
    of the winter of his going.

Scribbled me once, it's around somewhere or other,
word of their 'Edna Millay cottage' at Laugharne
saying come down to and disarm a while
    and down a many few.

O down a many few, old friend,
and down a many few.

Old Man Goes South Again Alone

O parakeets & avocets, O immortelles
& ibis, scarlet under that stunning sun,
deliciously & tired I come
toward you in orbit, Trinidad! – albeit without the one

I would bring with me to those isles & seas,
leaving her airborne westward thro' great snows
whilst I lapse on your beaches
sandy with dancing, dark   moist eyes among my toes.

He Resigns

Age, and the deaths, and the ghosts.
Her having gone away
in spirit from me. Hosts
of regrets come & find me empty.

I don't feel this will change.
I don't want any thing
or person, familiar or strange.
I don't think I will sing

any more just now;
ever. I must start
to sit with a blind brow
above an empty heart.